Through **THICK** and Thin and **Thick** Again

A Black Woman's Journey with BED (Binge-Eating Disorder)

Nettie Reeves-Lewis

ISBN: 1537286137
ISBN 13: 9781537286136
Library of Congress Control Number: 2016916460
CreateSpace Independent Publishing Platform
North Charleston, South Carolina

Endorsements

EATING DISORDERS ARE not just a white woman's disease. Nettie's willingness to courageously share her struggle with BED shines an important light on eating disorders among African American women. Her story uniquely speaks to African American women who know what it means to be thick and reflects many of the cultural issues and racial experiences that impact Black women's mental health, body image, and relationship with food. Nettie shares her poignant journey of self-reflection, self-discovery, and glimpses of her therapeutic healing process that ultimately led her to a place of healing and self-acceptance. With wonderfully insightful questions at the end of chapters, Nettie invites the reader to embark on their own journey of self-discovery and healing.

Gayle E. Brooks, PhD
VP & Chief Clinical Officer
The Renfrew Center of Florida
Coconut Creek, Florida

Nettie's brutally honest and transparent account of her experiences will awaken a needed conversation that often resides deep in the shadows of African American communities. Her poignant truths regarding the complicated relationships she endured with food, family connections, and her body image were simultaneously wrenching and encouraging. Somewhere between these pages you will find yourself identifying, connecting, and routing for her success. This is a brave piece of work as, at a minimum, it provides prompts to examine the intersections of our self-image, racial identity, and the internalized cultural oppression we continue to face within this society. Delightful read—it was inspiring and a testament of the indomitable spirit within us!

Dr. Mel Lewis
Practicing Clinical Psychologist
Davidson, California

Nettie Reeves's *Through Thick and Thin and Thick Again* is a brutally honest journey of how she not only endured life with an eating disorder, but how she managed to thrive in spite of it! As a practicing orthopedic surgeon, I counsel women on a daily basis about weight issues that are directly affecting their health. After working with these women for years, I have come to realize that the weight is not the main problem. It's the stress of caring for children, grandchildren, and husbands on a shoestring budget. It's the result of giving until there is nothing left for you. The problem is depression that manifests as a love affair with food. Thank you, Nettie, for this! Thank you for your courage to step out on faith and share your story, a story that so many African American women desperately need to hear. I believe that BED is a hidden epidemic in our communities, and this book is the first step in raising that veil of stigma.

Tamara Huff, MD
Board Certified Orthopedic Surgeon
Mayo Clinic Health System
Waycross, Georgia

Many of the women in our program had so many life obligations that fitness was not a priority for them. From the very first moment when the music began, the women were hooked. FUNky Fit put the "fun" in fitness for the ladies in our program! We saw a remarkable change in not only the fitness levels of our participants but also their mental and emotional states. The women had more confidence, were more open, and embraced FUNky Fit, because that one hour of exercise became their "me" time, which is something that none of the women in our program ever allowed for themselves.

Nettie Reeves's FUNky Fit is more than just an exercise program. While it does improve physical fitness, it also gave our women the courage to begin thinking about how to change their emotional, mental, and spiritual "fitness." Our ladies loved the program so much that some of them are no longer FUNKATEERS—they are now FUNKMASTERS! Thank you, Nettie, for this wonderful program!

Monica L. Alberti, MHA
Program Manager
Keep Moving, Keep Living
Mayo Clinic, Waycross, Georgia

Through **THICK** and Thin and **Thick** Again

A Black Woman's Journey with BED (Binge-Eating Disorder)

The mind, not the mirror, is the judge.

—Nettie Reeves-Lewis

Contents

Introduction

I HEARD A writer being asked by an interviewer why she wanted to tell her story. The writer proclaimed, "In the words of another writer, 'A person who likes to write stories is okay telling her girlfriends, but a writer has to tell the world.'" Being compelled to write has allowed me to heal. In order to heal, I had to be brutally honest with myself and dig deep, get emotionally raw and down to the bone. It has not been easy by any stretch of the imagination. But it was something that, for me, had to be done.

This book has been a fifteen-year process. It has taken everything I have to open myself up in such a way that you will come to understand when you read my story. After internalizing family secrets and sweeping them under the rug, my mind searched for outside help. What I found was an eating disorder.

There are things that happened in my life that, of course, involved my family members, friends, and others. Just as I couldn't have lived the stories without them, I can't tell the stories without them. Nothing has been written to initiate hurt or harm. Rather, it's for them to know that I've forgiven and moved on. Hopefully others will see that they too can heal from my exposure and honesty.

It was not God's will for me to write this book fifteen years ago, because all the processes hadn't taken place yet. I hadn't been around the full circle or experienced what I needed to in order to help others. I hadn't seen my way through. But for such a time as this, this book has come to fruition. And even as I began the process, I couldn't just sit and write like usual; instead I wrote some and stepped back, because it was severely painful and arduously draining.

For those who are dealing with any type of addiction, especially if you are an African American woman (or man) with BED, please journey with me. As you do, I pray that you will come to see your journey through the unrefined truth that only you can realize. And in doing so, I hope you will own your truth and allow it to be a healing mechanism. The questions at the end of chapters are designed to take you into that space. Keep in mind that you may feel uncomfortable, but you have to get to that distressed point in order to feel the relief that it will bring.

Finally, my struggle with binge-eating disorder was like a frightening tornado in the distance. I wanted to take cover at low ground but was instead drawn into the eye of the storm. I realize that my story and the picture of my life may be deemed severe to some and mild to others. But everyone has a story; here's mine.

Acknowledgments

I WOULD LIKE to give honor and thanks to Jesus, without whom my life would not be possible. He has seen me through many trials and brought me from a mighty long way. God, you will forever be my savior. You have put this book on my heart. Because of that, I can only do one thing: be obedient. I love you more than life itself.

Thank you, Eric. You are the light that always shines through. I couldn't have asked God for a more perfect husband to deal with my imperfections. I love you like a long walk along the beach.

Daniel, my son, you saved me. God knew that I needed you in my life to help me become a better Nettie. I wasn't a perfect mom, but because of you, I'm a better person. I love you "a whole lotta much!"

Momma, rest your soul; you were the epitome of strength. You did the best you could with what you had. I am forever grateful to you for bringing me in this world and teaching me right from wrong. I will always love you in spite of the many questions that are still unanswered. I miss your smile.

My sisters and brothers, we've been through it. Realizing that we too did the best we could with what we had, we are so blessed to have one another. I love you and still long for that closeness.

To my precious aunts and uncle, thank you. You have always given me the encouragement that I needed to live up to my full potential. You filled in some huge voids in my life. I love you for loving me.

To my N'shape family—what can I say? You have loved me through the many shapes, forms, and moves. In spite of it all, we're still together. Thank you for loving me for my talents alone. I love you like music in the air.

Thank you to the Renfrew Center for being there to provide the therapy that I needed to get to the other side. You saw in me what I had a hard time seeing in myself—especially my ability to help other women struggling with eating disorders through my story. You helped me see the light. I am grateful.

Finally, thanks to the many musical artists and recording groups that helped sustain my sanity throughout my life's journey. Music has been my lifeblood for as long as I can remember. For any given time, I can remember the songs that I sang during that stage of my life. It's the one constant that is in my blood, running warm through my veins.

1
The Thickness

"Herstory"

"**OH MY GOD!**" I shouted as I saw the cellulite on my arm. "How did this happen?" It seemed to start when I was about forty-nine years old, with the onset of early hormonal changes. But actually I remember it occurring on occasion during my first marriage, some ten years prior. Although I had been working out religiously for years, I still ended up with this lump of fat sticking out in my upper arm. I began to cry, not only because of the appearance but because I felt that I had done this to myself. I was taken over the edge with food as a consequence due to the pain of some choices I had made in life, especially the failed marriage. Even teaching ten to twelve hours of fitness per week didn't keep the weight from creeping. I took my hurt out on food.

Actually, it took it out on me. Any food. The foods that I taught others not to eat, I began to uncontrollably eat in secret, in hiding, in the car, in the closet, at night, in the dark—you name it. If it was the food of my choice—sweets and starches—I was on it. And I was on it until it was gone because of the insatiable appetite. After that, I wanted more. Then all of a sudden, I would hate myself for eating so much. I would ask myself, "Why did you do that?" And then other thoughts would enter my head on ways to get rid of it, like sticking my finger in my mouth or taking a laxative. Did I do those things? I never stuck my finger in my mouth, but I'm sure I took a laxative or two in my day.

After coming to my senses, I would realize that I have to be in front of a multitude of people to teach my own branded FUNky Fit group fitness (dance-based aerobics) classes. I was already getting paranoid because I knew I was going to look heavier, because I was going to be heavier. That alone caused me to want to eat more. My love-hate relationship with food was vicious. It's amazing how something that is required to live can also be the something that kills you.

The next day I awakened with hatred in my heart. Hatred for myself. "Not again! How could you do this to yourself…again? What is wrong with you? Okay, I'm going to do better today. Lord please take the taste of food out of my mouth. Don't let me get sick or anything, Lord. Just take the appetite away from me. I'm not going to eat any breakfast, and I'm only eating healthy foods all day long. Then I'm not going to eat anything after eight o'clock, because that's worked for me before, and I lost weight too. I know I didn't stick to it, but it worked, and this time will be different. I'm going to stick to it, starting today. Okay, now, what will I wear? I look too fat in everything. I don't understand how it can be so easy to put on weight and so hard to get it off. I'm going to have to get in three workouts every day this week."

The following day I would awaken with the same thoughts of "How can I unwittingly destroy myself?" It was getting more difficult to control my mind, and I blamed myself for not having enough will power to just stop eating! This occurred off and on for years, but I was always able to reel myself back in and control my weight through dieting.

But this time was different. I couldn't seem to get back on track. And it was worse than I had ever seen it. After working, I'd stop at the grocery to pick up healthy foods, but I would inevitably purchase some type of sweets and/or carbs. Before putting it in the basket, though, I would have an argument with myself about whether or not to put it in the basket. Eventually, it would wind up in the basket, and I'd tell myself that I would only eat one package of the four when I get home. As justification, I only had one packaged food in my shopping cart compared to a cart-full in most of the other folk's carts. Just walking to the car, I would think about where I would put the bag with my healthy *drug* in it. Another argument would ensue. "If I put it in the back then I won't be able to reach it." And I would have good intentions of doing just that. But as soon as I open the back door, I would throw the box into the front seat. I would tear the box open before I even left the parking lot. By the time I got home, all four of the packages would be eaten. And I would have thoughts of going back to get more. If not, I would eat whatever was in the house that was my drug (food) of choice: more carbs and more sweets.

I'd often tell myself the nuggets of information that I've told my students and clients, like, "Just go to bed." At this juncture, I wasn't able to heed my own advice. Nothing seemed to be working anymore.

After blowing up from a size ten to sixteen in four years (yo-yo dieting) and despising myself, I had reached my boiling point. My hypocritical feelings of myself was too much to bear. I knew what to do and had folks depending on me to help them. But it was apparent that I couldn't help myself.

It was a Friday afternoon, and I was home alone. I had eaten everything that I could get my hands on and was fighting with the notion of going to get more. Recently I had been drinking too—way more than I ever had before. But the liquor somehow eased the pain of my hatred for Nettie. I thought, "I'll be better off dead. This is no way to live. I should end it now!" Then I thought of my son, husband, and the grandchild who I hoped to have one day. "Something is really wrong with me. I think I have an eating disorder. But I don't have anorexia – there is no problem with me eating. And I don't have bulimia – I binge but I certainly don't purge. So I probably don't have an eating disorder. Maybe I can get the sleeve surgery, and that will help me get this weight off. Or go back and get some more diet pills, which don't really work anymore, so that won't make any sense. But maybe they'll work this time. I could take two a day instead of one." I perused the Internet to find info on getting bariatric surgery. I called a number from my phone."

The phone rang.

"May I help you?"

"Yes, I'm inquiring about weight loss surgery. Do you all have an orientation soon that I may attend?" I was desperate.

"Are you thirty pounds overweight?"

"Yes."

"Do you have an obesity related disease?"

"Like what?"

"Like diabetes or high blood pressure."

"Uh, no."

"Then I'm sorry, ma'am. You don't qualify for surgery."

I was at my wits end! "What! What am I supposed to do?" I thought. "I have to do something, or this is going to get real ugly."

Then it hit me. I should look for an overeaters' anonymous group or something like that. After frantically continuing to search, lo and behold, I could find none on the web that seemed credible. (This may have had something to do with my internal fight.) I kept searching, because if I didn't find something, I was going to lose it! I was already losing it.

Then something popped up called the Renfrew Center. It caught my attention, so I clicked the link. I read that it was a facility for eating disorders. I thought, "Oh, is this what I need? They probably can help me get this weight off!"

I called them and a polite voice on the phone answered. I told her that I would like to make an appointment because I needed help. She said they were closed for the weekend but she would have someone call me back on Monday. I wondered if she could hear the desperation in my voice.

Being at such a low point, I hung up the phone feeling lost and afraid. I felt that if I didn't find help and quickly, I would literally lose my mind completely. I stood in the shower crying profusely and praying until I was exhausted. Somehow I made it through the weekend—binging, this time, because I had hope of getting help. Although I continued to binge, the thought of that potential help eased my anxiety of committing suicide. "How did I get here?"

On Monday morning, the Renfrew Center called and arranged an appointment. A couple of days later, I was sitting inside the intake office speaking to a woman about my thoughts and feelings, and what I was experiencing at the time. I felt like I was in a bubble of some sort. I didn't know what to expect, and my mind began to wander. I felt big but seemed small. It appeared to me that everyone who was overweight must have the same issue that I had, including the ones that worked there.

"How can they work here and not get the help they need?" I was confused and in a daze, a maze that had no opening. I feared the unknown and the future. I didn't know if they could help me. If they could, then how? What were they going to do? "I don't see any blacks in here." The walls felt like they were closing in on me.

The intake specialist determined that I needed their intensive outpatient service. That meant that I would come in on two evenings per week and speak with the nutritionist, my therapist, and have group therapy. It also meant that I would have to eat a meal with the group and the nutritionist. The first meal was the hardest. As I sat around the table with the other young white girls, the nutritionist explained that we needed to choose a protein, a starch, a this, and a that. After everyone had gotten their meals, I noticed how hard it was for the other girls to eat. They had a problem eating enough while I was thinking, "Is this all I'm going to get to eat?"

The program seemed to be focused mainly on those who suffered from anorexia. That could be because not enough African American women seek the help that they need for BED. The administrators convinced me, however, that the program worked for those suffering from any and all eating disorders. In my group, I was the minority—the only black woman and one of two women in their prime. I was the only one suffering from BED.

It was the one-on-one time that I had with my therapist that made all the difference though. It had to be the most profound and eye-opening experience I've had in my life. Perhaps that's because it was the first time I had ever had the opportunity for someone to listen to just me, be interested in just me, be nonjudgmental about me, and empathize with me. It could also be because it was the first time that I needed help so desperately. For as long as I can remember, I was the one listening to others and giving advice. She prompted me to see things that had occurred in my life by asking simple questions, and most of all, listening empathetically. She knew that I felt I was to blame and had no answers for why I had this antagonism toward myself. She helped me figure it out and see things as an outsider looking in.

She said, "So tell me about Nettie."

I paused, began to cry, and said, "Oh man. Where do you want me to start?"

She said, "Start at the beginning."

I started off by letting her know that there were lots of wonderful things that had happened in my life. Many parts of my life, however, was catastrophic.

"Well, let's start there," she said.

Suddenly and reluctantly, I began to open up and dig way down deeply into my soul and told my most sacred secrets to a stranger that, curiously, I trusted.

It all began when I was growing up in the small town of Hopkinsville, Kentucky. The town was so small that when you entered it by car and began to spell it, *H-O-P-K-I-N*, by the time you reached *S*, you were out of it.

I don't really remember a whole lot about why we were thick. We just were a family of thick (heavy, fat, big-boned) girls. It could have been hereditary on my father's side. I recall my aunts were very tall and very big. They literally could be likened to Amazons, weighing in around 240 at over six feet tall. My brothers weren't heavy. That could be because they were encouraged to play sports at a young age. My oldest brother ran track, and my younger brother played baseball, football, and whatever else he could actively get his hands on. The girls, however, were taught to cook, clean, and play house, which is what I did. But all of us played outside—running, jumping, and skipping; playing hide-and-seek and hopscotch; and jumping rope. I absolutely loved playing outside and would stay out there until momma called us in, which was usually when the sun went down.

Momma knew I loved music and dance, too, so she would ask me to come and show her and her girlfriends the latest dance moves. I would demonstrate the funky chicken, mashed potatoes, and bus stop and make up a few of my own. I adored making momma smile.

I liked being in the spotlight. My siblings knew that too. Whenever it was time to take a picture or I got the opportunity to dance in front of people, I jumped to it. I don't know why that excited me, but it did. Perhaps it was the middle-child syndrome. My siblings, on the other hand, thought that I was being fast and a show off. "Nettie's always gotta show off. Nettie's always gotta be the first one in the picture. Nettie's always in the front," they would say.

It's too bad that dance studios, television talent shows, and the Internet weren't available back then, because I would've definitely been a star. Oh, and if my parents believed in me enough to support my dreams. With the ambition and unrestricted dreams that I had, I probably wouldn't have needed them.

"What else did you like to do as a child?" my therapist asked.

Cooking with my Easy-Bake Oven was pure joy and pleasure. I also liked the vanity with fake makeup that I received one year for Christmas. Making those cakes, spreading the icing and eating it was fun for me as a kid. My momma knew that. So much so that it was often used as a punishment tool. If I did something unappealing, I would not get that ice cream cone that was promised after dinner or the cake I baked in my oven. I thought, "How are you going to punish me with my own creation? That's my cake!" Or, "How can you let my brother eat an apple turnover and ice cream and not give me any? It's not fair! He never has to wash the dishes." In my opinion, that upbringing made everything that I did wrong in my eyes have a direct relationship with food. On the other hand, I was rewarded with food when I did something that was considered good—like bringing home a good report card, or making my bed. My emotional attachment to food created a permeable bond.

My therapist said, "When food has been embedded in you this way, it's not something that you can just use your will power on or pray away with. It becomes part of your DNA, your makeup, your upbringing."

It's how I was raised. That's why for most of the issues I face today, whatever goes on in my life, my obsession with food and how I relate to it, has everything to do with my emotional well-being. The more I was deprived of it, the more I wanted it. And so it is.

They say that you are a product of your childhood, and this could not be more true than in my case. In my mom's defense—rest her soul—she had no idea that she was causing me to have a love-hate relationship with food. She was doing the best she could with six children at the time. And if you think back to our African American history, food was a hot commodity. As slaves, we were certainly punished or rewarded with meals for getting work done or not. Obeying the master was absolutely the factor in whether or not you were going to eat. Momma raised me with that mindset. It was the only way she knew.

I remember my first taste of a banana. It looked so good as my brother was eating it. So I asked for one. Momma gave it to me. It was ripe, yellow, and angled just right. Momma broke the stem to get me started. My mouth watered as I peeled back the layers. I took my first bite and almost gagged. It tasted nothing like I had expected. It was slimy and soft, which I detested. I spat it out! Then I told momma that I didn't like it. She said, "People in Africa are starving. You're not going to waste any food in this house! Now sit there until you've eaten it—all of it."

Momma raised me the way she was raised and the way her parents had been raised before that. The days of whippings, lynchings, and runaways were still fresh when I was born in 1960. When one thinks of all they endured, it's a miracle that we (I) didn't end up with even more serious mental issues. So thank God for that.

In spite of my tumultuous relationship with food being developed in my younger years, I remember laughing and playing outside, taking trips to Beach Bend Park and the lake, spending time with extended family members on Sundays and Easters with my hair in Shirley Temple curls. But most of all I remember the music and the food.

"Herstory"

Every woman has a *herstory*. It's your history, your journey, your life. Let's do some soul searching to find out the source of your own individual relationship with food. Put real thought into finding your source and write down your answers below to the following questions.

Think about your childhood. Did you have a special relationship with food as a child like I did?

How was that relationship developed?

Were you deprived or rewarded with food?

What were the circumstances?

Growing Pains

The song playing on the radio was "Uptight (Everything's Alright)" by Stevie Wonder. Momma was making those fried apple pies. In those days they used lots of Lard, real butter, and white granulated sugar for cooking and baking. More than that, though, they were being eaten—every single day. There were mounds of jowl bacon, pig's feet, hog maws, chitterlings, pork chops and gravy, ribs, beef steaks and roasts, bologna, hot dogs, breads, potatoes, and mayonnaise. It's no wonder I used to hear old folks talk about somebody having "sugar." I now know that it meant they had diabetes. If you ate like that every day and then wash it down with sweet (and I mean sweet) tea, and then top it off with a homemade dessert, you would be a walking sugar cane too. But back then, who knew that the food was causing such diseases?

"Did you go to school?" my therapist asked gingerly.

I loved being in school, and we used to walk there every day. Although it was quite a hike for a child of eight, it wasn't that much of a caloric burn. What would burn more was the taunting that I endured from a fellow school mate. This girl, who lived in our neighborhood, was rough and tough. My heart would race as she would get the crowd fired up about beating me up. Why? Who knows! She probably doesn't know herself. What I have come to know, though, is that back then color meant something. My mother was part Indian (that's what they used to say if you were a pretty, brown complexioned Black, like momma). And daddy was light skinned with green eyes. Yes, he was mulatto which made us light skinned and "better than the darker people," so the darker people thought. (It blows my mind how enslavement and oppression was and is used to pit one people against each other.) So without question, that's why I was getting beat up and the crowd was so eager for it to happen. I didn't know it back then, but that was just the beginning of the fights and battles that would ensue due to my light complexion, and my relationship with food.

Nonetheless, it would put the fear in me like you wouldn't believe. Almost every day I could count on her calling me names from behind and daring me to knock a stick off her shoulder or cross the line that she had drawn on the street. I had to cross the line in order to get home! But that was her way of justifying a fight. I didn't want to fight. Just the thought of it now brings my heart to another beating level. I remember some days being so exhausted after making it home that I just couldn't do anything but eat. It was just too much and way too much for any eight-year-old to have to endure. My brother would stick up for me, but on those days that he walked with me from school, she didn't try to pick a fight. She knew he would jump at the opportunity to kick her tail.

One day without my armored brother around, there she was, with her cronies, all calling me names and making me nervous and fidgety again. But something happened on this day that was different than all the others prior. They were all shouting, "Nettie's eating cheese! Nettie's eating cheese!" I think that meant that I was afraid. Yep, I sure was. That was clear. But she got in my face that day and pushed me one time too many. I snapped. I pushed her back. I could hear the crowd yelling and making fighting gestures with their fists, like we were in a ring getting paid for the junior elementary welter weight championship. After pushing her back, she somehow stumbled to the ground. I'd like to think I did that. I got on top of her and didn't know what to do after that. So I pinned her arms down and just shouted at the top of my lungs, "Leave me alone!" I got up and ran home, picked up the phone, called momma (who was at work in her beauty salon), and yelled, "Guess what, momma? I got her! I got her down on the ground!" I felt good about my accomplishment too.

It's ironic though. On that day after talking to my mom and winning the fight, I still fought trying to find something to eat to take the pain away of being afraid, of winning or losing, of not knowing whether I would have to fight again, of the past and the future. Food just seemed to take it away. And I needed that relief, with or without the protection of my brother. It was obvious that he would not always be there to protect me but food certainly would be.

Growing Pains/Childhood

Perhaps you were like me and bullied in school. Maybe something happened to you that you feel is unthinkable or that is so vial that you cannot even think about sharing with others. Perhaps you feel too ashamed to talk about it because you feel it will hurt you more if you do speak about it. I'm here to tell you that as I write, I'm in tears. The pain that I endured as a child will rear its ugly head each time I think about it, and I think that no one else feels the same pain. Believe me, you are not alone. So take the time and reflect on what happened to you (and something happened to all of us) that made you nervous or feel the way I felt on those days walking home from school.

What in your childhood made you feel anxious or nervous?

When you felt this way, would you turn to food?

How would you feel once you'd eaten the food? better/worse/ indifferent?

Ain't No Sunshine

Although my family had its share of issues, like most families, we considered ourselves lucky to have both parents who worked. We lived in a home built from the ground and had the newest appliances and food on the table every day. I did not know that it was about to take a turn.

My parents divorced when I was ten years old, and we moved from the small town of Hopkinsville, Kentucky, to the big city of Louisville, Kentucky. Bill Wither's hit song was out at the time. It was entitled, "Ain't No Sunshine." Times were hard and the days of playing outside as well as being picky about what we would have to eat were gone. Just having food on the table was a welcomed gesture, and because we knew how hard momma worked to make that happen, we ate whatever she provided. Oftentimes, that was government cheese and other fattening, non-nutritious foods because it was the easiest to come by and the cheapest, or free. We often walked to school no matter how cold it was. Initially we moved in with a single mother and her children. Momma said she was our cousin, but I never figured that one out. She was nice but she talked really fast. It used to scare me how she disciplined her children. She would take her child's hand in hers and bend the fingers way back. Then she would take a long, hard, wooden ruler and beat their hands something fierce. I remember them cringing up on their toes as she hit them hard and as fast as she talked. They were terrified of their mother. It seemed that she would beat them for no apparent reason, too. Needless to say, it frightened me and my siblings enough to stay in line. I can still remember the cold, dark attic where we slept. Gone were the days of momma playing Motown records on the record player. I remember a transistor radio in the attic. And each time I hear Paul McCartney's, "Let 'Em In," it takes me back to that attic.

Eventually, for one reason or another, momma had enough of that, so we moved again. That would be one of many moves as momma waited for her name to be called for an apartment in the projects. Her name eventually came up, but that was after we had rented many cold, dark places; in some of these places we kept the milk cold on the outside staircase and awakened to the loud train on the viaduct next to the house.

As one can imagine, not only were our living spaces cold and dark, our affinity for each other as brothers and sisters was becoming cold and dark as well. We tried to survive individually and collectively as a family without parents. Too much friction, pain, and disagreements eventually caused the individuals to win out. Each one of us survived the best way we could.

"Sounds like your mom was having a hard time. Were you going to school during this time?" my therapist asked.

Yes. By this time I was in junior high school and living in the bricks of Southwick. I wanted to try out for the drill team. Although I was afraid, it took some real pushing (from God I think) to make me go for it. Deep down I really desired to see myself dancing on the team so, reluctantly, I showed up and tried out. And this was pretty typical of me. I thought I had enough guts, but I would get so very nervous that oftentimes when it came down to putting the wheels in motion, I just didn't have the courage to do it. But I went for it this time in spite of my MO of inadequacy.

My therapist said, "Well, that showed courage, didn't it?"

Yes, but in spite of my wanting it, I never thought I was good enough to have it. I thought the other girls were thinner and, therefore, prettier, because they were the ones who looked like society says women should look like, and they got the favors. I found this to be my MO all throughout the rest of my adolescent and teenage life. It was a running pattern. If other girls were skinny (or just smaller than me), I knew they would get the part, the opportunity, the guy, and I would be (once again) disappointed. It may not have stopped me from trying, but those intimidating thoughts kept me from believing in myself.

Nonetheless, I tried out for the team and made it! I was so excited, and that boosted my confidence. Oh boy, but wait. Now I have to contend with all these other girls and watch them with all their thinness (which was obviously on a greater scale than mine), looking at me as if to say, "What's she doing here?" And when I think back on it, I suppose I was prime for bullying. Wearing a size fourteen then is the equivalent of a size twenty-two today. I was heavier than most of the other girls. I always was. But more than that, I was just insecure. I didn't like myself much or how it or they made me feel. I wanted to be popular and liked by everyone. I wanted the cute boys to like me.

I remember the day of tryouts for drill team captain came up. Leading up to the day, I was anxious about trying out and thought that if anybody on that team could do it, I could. The day arrived, and I conveniently missed school. Whew! Now I have an excuse for not being captain, right. I wasn't there the day of tryouts. But, although I felt a sense of relief for not having to be rejected, I also felt disappointed for not showing up and applying myself. Knowing, too, that we couldn't afford the uniforms kept me from facing the embarrassment of not performing in the games. That inner struggle of being good enough and not being good enough still plagues me today. One of my favorite songs was a hit then. It was "Everybody Plays a Fool" by The Main Ingredient. I listened to it over and over again while I ate.

Each time I was invited to speak or appear on a broadcast or do anything that I claimed I really wanted to do, I second guessed myself. That same "drill team" fear popped up and reared its ugly head. If I felt confident about how I looked, then I tended to have confidence in my abilities. But if I've had a binging episode recently or even thought that I had gained weight, I tended to find excuses for just staying home.

"Where were your parents at this point in your life?" asked my therapist.

My mom was having serious issues of her own. So serious that it will take another book to write it all. But let's just say that she, unfortunately, wasn't in my life like a mother should be. As a matter of fact, my growing up without her full existence is another reason for my love for food. Not having the woman you idolized as a young girl help you through tough times that you didn't understand as a teenager can be a hard road to climb. I wasn't truly alone. I had my older sister, who took on the role of momma, and my other siblings as well. But when your household is in chaos (like worrying about where the next meal will come from or if the welfare check is going to come on time because you're already broke), the issues that you face as a child on a day-to-day basis (like being bullied or needing emotional security), seem unimportant.

And as mentioned, my parents divorced when I was only ten years old. Not that my father was around much, but at least there were two parents living in the home until then. Now I don't know if it matters much to have both parents if they were always fighting. Seems to me that my siblings and I might have been better off with just our momma, since together they were worse.

"What do you mean by that?" she chimed in.

I remember waking up to a screeching noise in the middle of the night. I followed the whining sound and light out of my bed, down the hall and into the kitchen. To my surprise there was my mother draped over my dad's lap as he whipped her as if she was a child. I'll never forget the look on momma's face as she looked up and saw me looking at her in that state. She tried to protect me by yelling, "Go back to bed Nettie!" It was too late. I had already been exposed. That was traumatic and something else I will never forget.

"That must have been hard to witness as a child," she stated.

Yes, it was. Aside from having traumatic experiences as a child like the ones I've shared—just not having a loving and nurturing family unit—was enough to turn to something outside of myself. My father worked as a Greyhound bus driver, so he was rarely home. My mother was an entrepreneur; she owned a beauty salon and ironically also worked as a nurse's aide in the mental institution in our home town of Hopkinsville.

They were always fighting about who was going to whip which child for misbehaving, or my uncles were over ready to fight my father for beating up my mother, or my mother was threatening to pour hot grits on my father. It was always something and something that children shouldn't have to try to process. It's hard enough for adults to process. But that was the life we lived.

Yes, it could've been the era in which I was born, too. It was the sixties, and black men, having been dominated for so long, felt their worth when being dominant over someone else; anyone. Unfortunately, that someone happened to be whoever was closest to them—their wives. And in this case, it was my mother, rest her soul. In spite of all that, my momma was wise and wanted a better life for herself and her children.

"What was your relationship like with your dad?" she asked.

I had indifferent feelings for my dad because I never really knew him. I remember a happy time that he allowed me to sit in his lap on the driver's seat and steer the car as he drove. But as a whole, I was more afraid of him than anything else. Momma loved to hear me sing, whereas he cared less. He chastised me for singing in the tub once because it was interfering with him watching wrestling on television. He came in and told me and my sister to keep it down. We did quiet down, but as little girls would naturally do, we started playing again; singing, splashing water, and giggling. The second or third time, he had had enough so he busted into the bathroom and beat both of us with a belt while wet and naked. What a dad.

Besides incidences like that, he never told me that I was pretty. I don't remember him hugging or kissing me, or anything that would resemble me taking on the role of a "daddy's little girl."

Ain't No Sunshine

As you can see, my dad was living in the home when I was a child, but he really was not there for me emotionally. Search your heart and answer these questions to give yourself a clearer picture of your relationship to your father.

Have you ever seen someone you love being abused?

What did that make you feel?

Did you grow up with your father in the home?

Did your father make you feel like you were "daddy's little girl?" If so, how?

If not, what do you wish he had done to make you feel more loved by him?

Life Lecture

By this time in the great city of Louisville, we recognized it wasn't the move we had anticipated it to be. Of course we all piled in the car and thought we were moving to Be-ver-ly. But Beverly Hills was way out in the far horizon for us. I'm glad that my mom left the situation she was in. Bless her heart, she tried to be a good wife and mother, working two jobs to make ends meet while living with my father who was also fathering plenty other children at the same time that we were being born. And prior to that, my blind grandfather permitted this man (her first alcoholic husband) to marry her when she was only thirteen years old. I often wonder if he sold her to the highest bidder. If not literally, it was certainly for him, one less mouth to feed.

Right before selling everything we owned and moving to Louisville, the strangest thing happened. Momma had this friend (or so-called friend) who came to visit. We were fortunate to have our grandfather live just a garden's length away. Literally, we would walk through the path in the garden to visit him and my aunt. I remember being over there hanging out with my aunt, which I loved to do, and someone running over yelling, "It's momma. Come quick!" So we all jumped up and ran through the garden, through the front door of our house, down the long ranch hallway, and into my mom's bedroom. I stayed back on the outside of the door with my little head piercing around the doorway. There she was lying across the bed just shaking like a leaf on a tree caught in a whirlwind. I was too young to understand what had happened to her but later in adulthood found out that that so-called friend, who had just left our house prior to us being summoned, was the first to give momma drugs. To this day I don't know if she was shaking because she had taken them or because she was already addicted and was having withdrawals. But that was the beginning of a whole new set of problems for momma and abandonment issues for me and my siblings.

"How so?" my therapist asked.

The abuse of diet pills continued. Momma would go from doctor to doctor to get them. And the doctors would write prescription after prescription. I know because I went with her on occasion. The steps leading to the doctor's office were made out of busted bricks. There was a screen door and then a front door, like on a house. The waiting room was cold and reeked of mildew. And there were people everywhere, all waiting to be seen. The nurse called her in. She and I went into the doctor's office and sat in a chair in front of his desk. There he was. A middle-aged, pot-bellied white man, sitting across from us with piles of files and papers everywhere. He was wearing a dingy doctor's coat and smoking a cigarette.

He asked her a couple of questions. "Are you taking the medication as prescribed?"

"Yes," momma said.

"Are you having any problems?"

"No."

Voilà! Prescription written and we were on our way to the pharmacist.

My therapist said, "That must have been something you remembered as you got older, huh?"

I didn't start putting this puzzle together until I was old enough to understand what had occurred to momma. All I knew then was that my momma was sick. I didn't even know whether the pills she was being prescribed were diet pills or that she was abusing them.

She would do really strange things like lay in the bathtub for hours and speak in tongue (or some language that only she understood) while slapping a drenched washcloth around wetting up the entire bathroom. On another occasion she went out in the middle of our neighborhood street naked, trying to stop cars. My brothers and sisters and I were always on edge because we didn't know what was next or when it would come. We were also totally embarrassed and ashamed. That's another reason that I felt inadequate. I didn't have the Leave it To Beaver home life and family relationships that I longed for or saw portrayed on television. This was a lot for me as a teenager, as well as for my entire family.

"Well, how was school going?" she asked.

The bullying continued in junior high. Since we moved around a lot I didn't know which school I would be attending the next time around. We moved from the area of the school that I liked (the drill team) so I had to attend the school that was designated for the new area. But this school I was well aware of, because it had a reputation of being awful. Folks said that the kids were bad and lots of fights occurred there. I begged momma not to send me to that school. By this time my armor (brother) was in high school. He was a year ahead of me.

In this particular classroom students sat across from one another, two by two. The teacher sat me across from two rough and tumble girls (I think they were girls) whom I was already intimidated by. We were to work on a project together. They lallygagged throughout the time we worked; laughing and playing around. It was obvious they weren't thinking about making the grade. I was, however. So I asked them something about the project. An argument ensued. Well, not really an argument. They said something. Then I said, "Just forget it." One of them said, "What! Fuck it?" I begged and pleaded with them that I didn't say that. And even though they knew those words weren't mine (my momma didn't play that), they used that to challenge me to a fight after school. Well, it wasn't really a challenge, either. They said, "Wait till after school, We gon' beat you up." I was terrified the rest of the day and school year. I hated that school.

Then my therapist said, "Your mom was doing the best she could, huh?"

In spite of momma's misfortune, she did her best to take care of us while she was struggling with her own demons. She was in and out of the hospital's psych ward many, many, many times. Whenever she would have an episode, and it was often, we would fight with one another on whether or not we should call the police. We knew that meant they would take her. And it was so hard to watch them put her in handcuffs and whisk her away as though she were a criminal. We didn't know what would happen to her after that. Eventually, we got used to it. Believe it or not, it got to the point when she was in the hospital, we got a bit of relief. And each time she would return home sobered up and well, we all would hope (perhaps falsely) that she was healed and that was the last time we would endure that pain. As a matter of fact, back then I thought that she suffered from mental illness. But it was overdosing on the diet pills (and perhaps other prescribed drugs) that caused her manic behavior, which eventually may have caused some mental illness.

"That had to be tough on the entire family," my therapist proclaimed.

As you can imagine, this put a tremendous strain on me and the rest of my family. Each of us learned to cope and deal with it the best way we could. As I've come to understand my family's dynamics and makeup, I see that each of us were dealing, in our own ways, with these traumatic experiences that we endured as children.

Life Lecture

As a black woman dealing with binge-eating disorder, or one whose loved one is, can you see a family dynamic that could have left you or your loved one coping the best way you/she could?

Without blaming others, what would you like to say to the disorder?

Can you think about forgiving who or what you consider to be the culprit of the basis of your binge-eating disorder?

How can you take the first step at forgiving yourself?

Fake It Until You Make It

In high school, I became that somewhat popular girl who I always wanted to be, in a decent school of course. My body naturally thinned out somewhat, but I still had body-image issues and feelings of inadequacy. I just faked it, and made it the best way I knew how. I built up enough confidence to go out for things like Prom Queen, but when I didn't win I wasn't surprised; upset and embarrassed, but not surprised. It was always going to be the prettiest girl who drove to school in her own car, wore the baddest rags, whose face was always creamed, and who knew all the guys and other popular girls. No matter how much I wanted it, that was not going to be me. So I kept faking it until I made it.

After graduating high school, I couldn't even think about college because we had no money. Besides, no one talked about going to college. It was a major accomplishment to finish high school. So I applied for and began working for the University of Louisville's payroll department. (Had I known the value of a college degree, I could have taken classes for free because I was a full time employee.) Back in 1978, you could get a good job with a high-school diploma. And Lord knows I needed to work so I could afford to get clothes, a car and all the other "things" that would make me feel worthy and normal. And I wanted to help momma too. I was working in the day and partying at night. Envisioning myself and making headway to get out of my circumstance was in the horizon. One of the hottest songs in the club was "Boogie Oogie Oogie" by A Taste of Honey. Hearing it loud while on the dance floor took me to other places.

Shortly after making my own salary, I decided to go to modeling school to become one of the girls in the magazines that I often admired. I spent my own hard-earned money to get my headshot and composites done, to take runway and print classes, and to graduate from Cosmo Casablancas. Now I was on my way to making it big. I was going to be a model in magazines, on television, and on the runway, who were beautiful and glamorous and loved by everyone.

"But wait. There are no models in those mediums who look like me; none of them wear a size fourteen to sixteen, none of them have self-esteem issues, none of them have cuts on their arms," I thought. So I went on my first real diet because I thought that if I could get thin enough, it would solve all my problems. I did get down to like a size twelve.

I had to get my weight down because if I did, then maybe I could be the one that the agency would choose as the next "it" girl. If not, I could settle for being that one plus size model. "I'm okay with that." I told myself that I could be the one that everybody wanted to be like. And I'm going to be thin and a great looking model at whatever cost. I already had the face not a Halle Berry face but definitely a Vanessa Williams face. People used to say that I looked like her. Yep, I'm going to be just like the models in the glamour magazines and even the housekeeping ones—rich and famous. Um hmm! You know the ones on the billboards with hardly any clothes on. Yes, those who have the men drooling over them and women wanting to go to any lengths to look like them. I'm going to be that girl and losing this weight is my ticket.

"So that's where you think the dieting started?" my therapist asked.

Little did I know that that was the beginning of the roller coaster ride of my life. On one hand I wanted to look like those models but on the other I wondered why they all had to look like that. Knowing it was virtually impossible for me to achieve, I thought I could be the one to change the industry.

Needless to say, the agency just took my money, along with a host of other girls, none of them were what clients were looking for in models back then. It was the age of Twiggy. Little did I know, in my current state, I would never have measured up. They were in business to make money. It didn't matter if dreams would be shattered, or what one endured to put themselves in a capable space of acceptance. Sure, I got a few jobs around town, passing out cigarettes at concerts and the like. Although that was far from where I wished to be, I never gave up hope that the stones would lead to the top.

"Sounds like there was a little bit of love-hate relationship going on with yourself?" she questioned.

It's ironic that although I felt inadequate about myself, I must have projected myself in another light. You see, the other girls who lived in the projects saw me as a threat. They thought that I had it going on. They felt that I had ambition and drive; something they didn't have. So it was no wonder that crazy things happened to me while living in Southwick.

I was in two fights. One because the girl across the street liked a guy who lived a couple of doors down from us who she heard liked me. I knew nothing about it. She and some girls came to our front porch and knocked on the door. I thought she was calling me to come hang out. But when I walked out the door, I was ambushed! She had a knife. And she cut my arm. Luckily, I was able to get back in the house before she killed me. It was a frightening experience. I never expected she would do that to me.

Another fight was with the girl who lived right next door to us. She was known to abuse drugs and was often out of her head. One day she was calling momma names and saying hurtful things about her to me. I didn't know how to process that so I lashed back out.

Then she lashed at me with a darn knife! I know. My thoughts as well! Who does that? She cut me on the other arm. Now I have both arms scarred up and am very self-conscious about them. There went my dreams of being in the magazines.

When people asked what happened I would lie and say that I scratched my arm on a clothes hanger or something like that. Anything to not say I was cut in a fight, because people would then judge my character. Of course, I had already prejudged myself. And I had enough to try and defend already. Since then, I have applied every product under the sun to ease the appearance of those scars. Even though they have somewhat dissipated, the scars inside are nice and fresh.

My therapist chimed in, "Yes. I can imagine they are. That was a lot to get through."

I consistently endured taunts of having a flat butt and a crazy momma and the likes. But there was something inside that drove me to want more, be better and do better than those I lived around with. While they cooped up inside one of their homes (or ours) playing cards, I would work, or try to find something that would make me feel like I was normal and get me out of my situation.

Every family that lived in Southwick was dysfunctional, each separate from the rest. That was our reality. I lived inside of a dysfunctional family, but that didn't mean that I had to be dysfunctional. While young and naive, I didn't realize that life could be different. That was my reality. But when I got older, I saw a huge difference in where I was and where I wanted to be. It was someplace, any place, different from there. So I continued to fake it until I could make it.

Fake It Until You Make It

Sometimes in life, we have to do what is necessary to survive. I call it faking it until making it.

Have you ever felt like you had to lie in order to protect yourself?

Have you ever felt that you had to fake it to make it?

Explain what you felt you had to do.

The Men All Pause

In 1979 as my girlfriend and I were walking to my car after an Earth, Wind & Fire concert, with "After The Love Has Gone" still ringing in our ears, I met a guy. He was tall, slightly bow legged, light skinned and had curly hair. I really couldn't believe that he liked me. But he did. He had just graduated high school (I graduated the year prior) and was on his way to play basketball for a junior college in Illinois.

We began talking (that's what we called dating) and spending time together. We became intimate, and I knew that he loved me. I was learning more and more about his family and how they lived. Meeting them made me realize that functional families could have dysfunctions. They didn't have our set of issues, but they certainly had their own, like all families. It wasn't long after he moved to Illinois that he asked me to come live with him. Without saying the words but feeling the need (it was my ticket out of Southwick), I took it. Maybe I fell in love with the idea of getting away from the stress and turbulent life that I had. A new start was in order. Oh, and I did love him too.

He was from a good family with both his mom and dad at home. And they were very good people. The one thing they did very well was support their children. So they agreed for me to move to Illinois. They supported us as I worked and he went to school—- well, played ball. We had fun there; cooking and partying with friends, hanging out at the games, and driving home to Louisville and back whenever we could.

That was my first dose of life outside my own set of brick walls. I liked the feeling of what the outside world had to offer. A year later I was pregnant with my son. His mom suggested I come live with them so she could help me take care of him. I was twenty years old and didn't know what else to do. So I agreed. Eventually he quit the basketball team, left school, and came back home too. We had our beautiful baby boy. But that was just the beginning of a rocky ten years with a man who just couldn't quite grow up as fast as my son, and I needed him to. I gained eighty pounds during my pregnancy.

After ten years of that rocky road, I hung up the basketball sneakers, if you will, and finally decided to move on. Mind you, all throughout the ten years, there was mega fun and mega pain; breaking up to make up and breaking up again. We were young and dumb. Eventually, we broke up for good.

A few years before our final breakup, however, when our son was around six, I decided that I needed to go to college to generate a better quality of life for him and myself. I consistently encouraged his dad to do the same, but for some reason he didn't see life the way I did. Perhaps it was because he didn't have to. After working two jobs and going to school, I graduated in 1991; the first in my family to graduate college. My son's grandmother (his dad's mom) was very instrumental in the four years it took me to graduate by watching over him while I worked, attended school, and played.

I have taken heat over this in my own family because I had help from her. They somehow felt that I should have felt the full burden of having a child, instead of being happy that I had the help. And I allowed them to make me feel bad for not, as they say, "raising my own son," (I've often been told that I needed to develop thick skin). But both my son and I knew better. I did raise him. I taught him to have respect, manners, and life skills. I taught him how to treat people and have integrity and honesty. And I loved him with all my heart. Was I perfect? No. And I was young. I was basically a mere child myself.

Our son has grown into the fabulous young man and husband I always prayed he would. I eventually, from a distant city, helped him acquire his driver's license, a car, a college degree, and most of all, good health. His dad married another woman and has three children. Such is life.

"Sounds like you kind of knew what you wanted to do at this point in life." stated my therapist.

I think it was at this point in my life that I sort of suppressed all of my childhood experiences and tried to move on with my life as if none of the past had happened. I wasn't apart from the facts of my life, but I considered myself free of it and put the past behind me. Also, these were issues that I would never speak to anyone about because I didn't want that to be my life.

She said, "Okay then. Let's move on."

I met another man, a preacher, in 1993 while looking for a place to teach my newfound love of Jazzercise. He asked me out. I obliged. About a year later, we began to plan a wedding. He was from South Carolina—an ex-football player turned pastor. He wanted to move back to the South, and I wanted to move to the South because I heard that Charlotte, North Carolina, was going to be the next great city to live in. At the time, in 1994, Atlanta was the hot city to live in for blacks because of better opportunities. My song was "Breathe Again" by Toni Braxton. According to my momma, "Every song is your song, Nettie!" She was right.

The question from my soon to be husband was "What are you going to do with your son?" This was (and is) a very delicate subject matter for me. I didn't think that should have been a question. Then after being somewhat coerced, I deduced that he should probably stay with his dad in Louisville. He was fourteen, and going through some things that now I know was puberty. His dad and I talked and decided the best thing would be for him to stay in Louisville with his dad since he was at that stage and needed him more than ever.

I thought that his dad was ready for the responsibility, and I wanted them to have the relationship that a dad and son should. So I agreed. I have to admit that the slight nudge from my soon to be preacher husband helped me make that decision too. He had a son by a previous marriage and often talked about how it feels not to have your child with you. Shortly after we had married and moved, I was moping around and crying because I missed my son. He said, "See how it feels?" For some reason, I felt that he wanted me to feel what he felt. And I did.

This, out of all the things in my life, is the biggest regret of my life. Although I spoke with other women who did the same thing, it left an emptiness inside me that to this day I cannot shake. I don't know why I had some sense of delusion. When our son was a little boy, one of the ills that I had with his dad was that he never spent time with him. Even when our son was at his home, his mom would take care of him. So I conveniently thought that this would finally allow him to be the dad that I knew he could be and his son needed him to be. But he did eventually grow up, allowing our son to live with him and his wife for four years when I moved to Charlotte. I suppose they did the best they could too. I appreciate her for allowing my son to live in her home.

On the other hand, momma loved the condo that my son and I lived in prior to my leaving Louisville. She wanted to live in it when I moved, so I allowed it. I paid the mortgage for the next ten or so years, so she wouldn't have to be concerned about where to live. I continued to pay it even after my sister moved in with her, rent free.

"Okay, so you obviously loved your mom and your family. You also had discovered working out by now. How did you feel about your body?" she asked.

By this time I had discovered diet pills and was able to keep my weight down either with them, fad diets or both. I may have gone to the same doctor that my mom went to at some point. When I moved from Louisville to Charlotte to start a new life with my new husband, I felt like I was in a good place; traveling yet again to a new beginning, allowing weight to dictate my mood.

"Did you remain in contact with your family?" she asked.

After living in Charlotte a while, I remember people asking me if I were an only child. I would like to have thought that was the case because I acted so independent. A more realistic explanation is because I never spoke of some of my siblings unless prompted to. I think it's because what we went through tore us apart. We were not close like I wished. I often longed for us to have get-togethers to laugh and reminisce. I suppose there was nothing to sit around the camp fire and talk about unless it was bad memories. We did have good ones too, though. My brothers and I often do reminisce. But for some strange reason, my sisters liked hearing about my misfortunes. If they weren't true, they seemed to make some up. Again, I chalked it up as being the middle child who just didn't fit in. But I often felt like the black sheep, which perpetuated my feelings of being unwanted and needing to find something to rely on. (This was another way in which being oppressed affected black families—giving labels such as "black sheep" implying waywardness and outcast.) Others think it was just plain old jealousy.

"Well, how was the marriage summing up?" Another question from my therapist.

Little did I know preachers could be so selfish. My first encounter of this characteristic was on our honeymoon. We were coming back from Hilton Head and stopped at the convenience store. I was about to come in with him when he yelled, "What do you need to come in for! Just stay in the car!" I thought, "Did I do something wrong?"

That was the beginning of five years of hell of dealing with a Jekyll and Hyde personality—freshly married, in a new city, without my son, and miserable. But I was going to be a good wife because I took those vows seriously. Being married meant the world to me, and I knew that effort had to be put into it.

"Tell me about those five years," inquired my therapist.

It just so happens that he (we) came to pastor a church that was undergoing major parishioner reconstruction. The corporate United Methodist Church wanted and needed the church to better reflect the neighborhood in which it stood. Whites (who founded the church and who used to live in the neighborhood) had moved away, and blacks were now residing in most of the area. However, the whites would drive back in to attend church on Sundays. In other words, people who lived in the neighborhood were not attending the church. There were petitions, injunctions, and all kinds of other tactics to keep us from leading the church. They would rave about how well he spoke but did not want him to lead them.

Due to the turmoil, we could never seem to get our marriage together. We were both focused on the church. I took up the slack for everything from singing in the choir, leading the usher board, running summer camps, typing and folding all the bulletins at 2:00 a.m. on Sunday mornings, to developing women's day programs. I even worked a full-time job at the bank and went directly to the church to teach a Jazzercise class, then went home and cooked steak dinners while he sat with his feet propped up watching television and dipping snuff—something that surprised me because I didn't know he did that.

I often wondered, "What have I done." Whenever he had an issue, he seemed to take it out on me. There are many stories of which I can tell that made me feel that way. One Thanksgiving we were invited to my aunt's home in Chicago. I already felt somewhat estranged from my family, so I really wanted to go. He agreed that we would go, and we did. It was very cold and snow was everywhere. You could hear the wind whistling outside the windows. We had also agreed to stay with my aunt. I was excited because I adored her (and still do). When we arrived at her home, I could tell that something was wrong with him. He was moping around and just not engaging like I would had it been his aunt. I could tell he was unhappy; my aunt could too.

After constant moping by him and probing by me, he informed me that he was mad at me because I didn't order us a car and a hotel room. I was like, "I thought we agreed to stay here." It didn't matter. The argument continued. So like a good little wife, I got out the yellow pages and started calling around for a car and hotel room.

As you can imagine it was an adventure trying to find either because of the holiday. After spending painstaking hours on the phone (time that should have been spent with my aunt), I did finally find an expensive hotel room, but no car was available in the entire city. There we were in a cab, off to the hotel; spending money that we didn't have. My aunt was upset, but she had a very mild way of showing it. I was upset, because I wanted to spend that time with my aunt. But more than anything, I wanted to please him. When we got to the hotel, that's when he let me have it. And I mean, he let me have it. He cursed me out. I tried defending myself by talking back and stating what our original plans were. His arm drew back and hit me in the jaw with his fist! I didn't know what to do.

"What did you do?" my therapist asked fervently.

I just broke down and cried like a baby, because I couldn't believe he hit me. I was in physical pain but the feelings of betrayal were beyond belief. He never said he was sorry. That night, we slept on opposite ends of the bed, as we often had.

The next day was acting day—Thanksgiving. It was also my birthday. My uncles and cousins were there from Louisville. I had to put on a happy face but they, of course, could tell that something was hugely wrong and that I was unhappy. They realized I wasn't the bubbly girl they knew.

"Is that when you decided to leave him?" she asked.

No, I remained in the marriage, trying to work it out long after that. But I looked in the mirror one day and thought, "I look so old." I could see the wrinkles creeping in. Being married to him was aging me fast. On top of that, I was turning back to food to ease the pain. I also saw a wrinkle of cellulite in my leg and busted out into tears, again.

I found a weight-loss doctor in Matthews. I really didn't want a prescription for diet pills but just to know if there was something wrong with me. I thought maybe she could tell me what kinds of foods to eat in order to lose the weight that I desperately needed to lose. She took a ton of tests. When she called me back into her office to get the test results she told me that I was the pillar of health, except for one thing. She said, "Your thyroid is not producing any hormone at all and that's why you're not losing weight in spite of teaching five aerobic classes per week." I was like, "Okay, so what does that mean." She said, "I'm going to give you a prescription for hypothyroidism called Synthroid and I need you to take it exactly as prescribed." I said, "Okay. How long will I have to be on it?" She said, "For the rest of your life." What! You gotta be kidding me.

I was shocked but I finally discovered why my hair was thinning, and why I was always cold. So much so my fingertips would turn blue after exposure to just a little bit of cold. In addition, my heart would flutter at times, my skin was extremely dry, I couldn't muster up energy, and of course, I consistently gained weight.

Here I am thinking that I'm healthy; I eat a decent diet, work out like crazy and I'm actually unhealthy? And I have a disease, nonetheless? I felt in my heart of hearts that I created my thyroid problem. Although I had no proof, I was under the impression that I was to blame due to my weight fluctuations. And because of the hatred for myself, it too, triggered me to binge.

So, after five years of the pressure to remain thin and pretty for the front pew; losing my voice singing high soprano, taking the brunt for everything from disgruntled choir directors to chatter behind my back of him cheating, I had had enough. I left him while he was on a trip to see his son in upstate New York. It was one of the many journeys he made to New York. However, it was my third time making the journey to leave him. And this time would be my last. Oh, by the way, there were a lot of hymnals that come to mind during this time of my life. I'm usually in church when I'm reminded of them.

The Men All Pause

I learned from my mother that taking care of your man should be your number one priority. It often times meant that I would sacrifice my own needs for theirs.

Have you ever been in a relationship that you felt like you were the only one trying to hold it together?

How did that make you feel?

Explain how that behavior may have contributed to your relationship with food.

Water into Wine

Prior to leaving my ex-husband, I had been teaching Jazzercise at the church for about four years. During this time, I trained two other women to become instructors. One of them often alleged that she "wanted to be me." I took it as flattery but not literally. When I decided to leave my husband and go to Louisville until I could determine what I wanted to do, I agreed to leave my business in her hands in case I wished to return. I wanted my students to continue working out and to take care of themselves in spite of my not being there.

I left my music, stage, rolodex, and everything else to her hoping it was secure. She promised it would be. We had built trust over the years. I went to Louisville and to Chicago to get my head on straight.

In the end, I determined that Charlotte was big enough for both me and my ex-husband, so I began to make preparations to come back to what I called home. I proceeded to call her to let her know that I would be returning.

At this time my son was nineteen years old. Again, I tried to get him to move to Charlotte with me. But again, he refused. He liked his life in Kentucky.

I had secured an apartment without a job, and everything else was lining up and falling into place. I felt that God was in it. I called her at work over and over only to be given one excuse after the other as to why she could not come to the phone. Eventually, it hit me that she was purposefully avoiding me.

I moved back to Charlotte, moved into my brand new apartment and was ready to get my Jazzercise classes back. Weeks passed as I continued contemplating on how I would reach this trust worthy friend who would never answer my calls.

One evening the doorbell rang. I answered the door to an unknown person who handed me a certified letter. He didn't say anything but, "Are you Nettie Reeves?" When I answered, "Yes," he handed me an envelope. I carefully opened it. There it was, a letter of termination from Jazzercise. Okay, now why is Jazzercise terminating me? It's been my world for the past six years. I brought it to Charlotte and introduced fitness to the black community of women. It was like my religion. So I cried my eyes out with a pit in my gut because I knew that somehow that so-called friend who wanted to be me, who avoided all my calls and had all my stuff, had something to do with this. And she proceeded to teach my classes as I continued to be devastated and hopeless.

"I can certainly understand you being devastated and hurt behind that," my therapist asserted.

It was about a week or two later that the phone rang. The voice on the other end said she was the fitness director at a women's gym which was right across the street from my apartment. She said, "I heard that you're the best doggone instructor in Charlotte, and we want you to come teach for us." Oh my God! You can just imagine my joy in hearing that. But now what? I don't have my own routines. All I've done is learn routines that have already been choreographed (although I often said that I could do that myself). Now I have to!

I went upstairs to my desk and started working. I created my business name, logo, and plan. Then I began to choreograph my first routines for N'shape with 'N's FUNky Fit. That was in 2000. The first song I choreographed was "Maria Maria" by Carlos Santana.

I also got my job back at the bank. Now I was cooking at five hundred. I felt real freedom for the first time in my life and realized that everything that I had been through with my ex-husband was to feel what I felt right then, right there. My divorce was final. My weight was stable because the medication was regulating my thyroid. Of course I was working out, but now creating and dancing; doing what I loved to do, on my own terms, with my own business.

Water into Wine

Blessings in disguise are a welcomed relief from circumstances that may have us swirling out of control.

Have you ever felt like there was a reason for some misfortune that happened in your life?

What was the misfortune?

What was the good fortune that resulted from going through it?

2
The Thinness

Short but Sweet

HAVING CREATED A new life for myself, I felt on top of the world. This time not because of the stake I had in a man but because of what God had granted me. I discovered my talents. I was writing and producing plays, and sometimes I starred in them too, reminding myself of Spike Lee. Each play was the highlight of an eventful gala that consisted of a high fashion show, food, drinks, and plenty of elegance. This actually began at the church as a Women's Day program that was dumped in my lap after the initial organizer quit.

My work as a philanthropist was rewarding as I was able to acquire Elizabeth Catlett works of art for the Mint Museum of Art in Charlotte. Google describes her as "an African American graphic artist and sculptor best known for her depictions of the African American experience in the twentieth century, which often had the female experience as their focus." I also found an increasing love of fitness, and I practiced my newfound admiration of nutrition as I helped others reach their full potential.

Suddenly, my body began to get really tight and toned. I lost about thirty pounds and went from my normal size fourteen to sixteen to a size eight to ten. At one point I got down to a size six. I was teaching FUNky Fit, and training myself and others as it had become my full-time business and passion. It was so successful that it took up all of my time. I had to make a choice of whether to run the business or write and produce plays. I was in the process of writing my tenth play at the time. But because it didn't pay the bills, I chose the fitness route with hopes of one day getting back to my other love of writing.

"It sounds like you found your calling," said my therapist.

Life was good for the next seven or so years (from 2001 to 2008) as my business grew exponentially. During this time, I received awards for the number of people I was able to help and the community work I did, one of which was the Steve Harvey Hoodie Award (a.k.a. Neighborhood Award). I was on the cover of local magazines, and stories of my accomplishments were also in national magazines and articles. I was finally living my dream of being inside magazines.

"What do you think made you so successful?" she asked.

One of the major things I told my potential clients was, "I will help you but I don't believe in quick fixes—no diet pills, no shots, no starving." Most didn't know that I had had experience with all of that. That's why I knew it didn't work. It was also the time that gastric bypass surgery had become popular, and I had clients who still tried to eat like they did prior to having the surgery. I had firsthand experience in knowing that unless the mind was changed, the body would be the same. That brings me to my business motto: The mind, not the mirror, is the judge. That was never truer for anyone more than it was and is for me, then and now.

Shortly after coming back from receiving my award from Mr. Steve Harvey, I attended the Pride Awards which is a local awards program where recipients are honored for their work. I received that award as well. It was humbling. My speech was dedicated to my mother who at the time had been suffering with Alzheimer's, and it would have meant the world to have her or some family there to celebrate with me. But as usual, my N'shape family was there to support. I was grateful.

That night, after the ceremony had ended, I walked through the front doors. There, I met the man. There he was standing there; a tall, dark, handsome specimen. It was sort of the weirdest thing I'd experienced because as our eyes met, I remember him reaching out his hand to shake mine. Then I remember saying, "Thank you" to his "Congratulations." But it seemed like thirty minutes had passed. I walked on, puzzled. That night I thought about him often, wondering who he was, even though it had been ten years since my divorce and I was now married to my career.

Each year after the Pride Awards on Saturday, the Martin Luther King Jr. breakfast is scheduled for the following Monday. I hadn't been in years. One of the seniors that I taught whom I called mom, asked if I wanted to attend with her. She had an extra ticket. I said sure and there we were at 5:30 a.m. off to the event. We walked through the same doors that I met that man at the Pride Awards. (Yes, it was the same venue.) And who was standing in the very same door? That same man. He said, "Hi! Do you remember me?" I said, "Of course I do." He didn't waste any time getting my number this time. And after many tries to get me to take the time off work to have lunch with him, we finally did. We've been together since.

"What a great story!" She said.

"So you found the right man. Did the business continue to grow? And how were you feeling about your weight at that time? Oh, and did you have a favorite song?" asked my therapist.

In spite of the small concern the country had for an economic downfall, I moved into my own fitness studio (building) in 2006. It had my name stamped on the wall. My favorite routine at the time was "Sexy Back" by Justin Timberlake.

After spending almost a hundred thousand dollars to get it up-fitted and ready, I was planning to be there for a long time. I had a great following that I had built from scratch. As a matter of fact, I was the first black aerobics instructor in Charlotte to "own her own business" in the sense that I wasn't working for a gym or the YMCA. I wanted to have control over my classes. So I rented out gymnasiums and packed the house with one hundred to three hundred Funkateers (students) per class. They would be lined up around the corner and out the door to attend. The charge was five dollars. I had made it, and my weight was staying down, naturally. I was both pleased and panicked at what I had created.

After three years, I felt compelled to offer the community more than just classes, (and needed to because we were busting at the seams) and many students asked me to consider expanding so that they could attend more often. Since I could afford it (with the help of some really good friends), I pursued my own facility.

3
Thickness Again

Life Happens

BETWEEN 2008 AND 2010, the economy was plummeting. People were losing their jobs, and the first thing they stopped paying was their gym fee. Love goes a long way until it begins to affect the wallet. That meant me. Then, this craze called Zumba began to get popular, and it seemed that everyone, except my diehards whom I love dearly, wanted to do it instead of FUNky Fit. It was new, and there were classes being offered on every corner. Again, if it was closer, that meant less gas, and time in traffic. It felt like I was a mom-and-pop grocery store who went the extra mile to make my customers happy, time and again. Then Walmart moves into the neighborhood, and suddenly all my customers are never seen again.

Even many FUNky Fit instructors whom I had trained—a lot of who learned everything they could from me under the auspices that they would be FUNky Fit instructors—either started their own thing using my model or started teaching Zumba using my model. Also, I was instrumental in jumpstarting fitness programs at large corporations, and because my business needed full attention and I couldn't be there at their beck and call (like I was prior to leasing my building), they deserted me. All of that hurt my business and my heart.

"It sounds like you helped a lot of people along the way. I know how it feels when you've been hurt and betrayed." she said.

My body was also hurting. Besides the hot flashes, lack of sleep, mood swings and emotional turmoil that triggered me to eat, around this time, I was feeling excruciating pain in my right leg and sometimes both. I had been feeling it off and on for a couple of years, but it was getting much worse.

One day, my girlfriend and I decided to go check out the new store called Ikea. When we got there my leg was already hurting, and I knew that I wouldn't be able to stand for very long. But when we got inside and began to walk around, we discovered that there was only one way out. To get to that exit, you had to walk the entire store consisting of three levels. I knew then that I had to do something about the pain. I almost died that day. And that was the first and last time I ventured into Ikea.

The pain got to be so severe that I would pray not to end up in a wheel chair. I sought the help of a neurologist because it was determined that the pain was deriving from my back. A spine specialist gave me shots of medication directly into the affected nerve on three separate occasions, and even that didn't help. After that, many drugs were prescribed, but I refused to take them. The only alternative, according to them, was surgery. They even scheduled the surgery date, which I refused, because they had told me all the succeeding problems I could potentially have after surgery, like more surgeries to replace pins.

It's ironic that the only time the pain would subside was during my teaching FUNky Fit. However, sure enough, the weight continued to climb. The stress of it all was too much, but I dealt with the pain; continuously praying for healing for another three years.

Then one Sunday my husband and I were in church. Our pastor mentioned that he was going to pray for healing. He asked everyone who was in pain to stand up. My legs were killing me, but I humbly stood anyway. I remember once again begging Jesus to please take the pain away. As you can imagine, the pain continued after the prayer, although I did have hope that it would miraculously disappear.

After church, my husband and I needed to stop at Bed Bath and Beyond to pick up one item. He asked me if I wanted to go inside with him or stay in the car (which I often did when I was in pain). Something told me to go in. And I did. As soon as I walked in, my eyes were drawn to a large display of knee pillows. The sign read, "Rid Back Pain Naturally." What did I have to lose? We each got one. I slept with it that night and haven't had nerve pain since. I'm convinced that God healed me that day.

In the midst of my nerve pain, my annual pap smear came back from the lab with abnormal cells. There went a round of more tests and biopsies and then a hysterectomy. Because I was in such good shape, my doctor said that I could get back to teaching classes within a couple of weeks. I taught, but it didn't stop me from continuing to gain weight. The stress of it all was too much to bear. I remember creating a routine to "Bust Your Windows" by Jazmine Sullivan. It felt like my world had busted.

Life Happens

Physical pain takes you completely out of your game. It can prevent you from having a quality life.

Have you ever experienced physical pain that worried you?

What was the diagnosis?

How did you move past the pain of worry and move on with your life?

Death Happens

My mom was in a nursing home, and my sister, who lived close by, rarely went to see her because it pained her to see momma in such a devastated state. This devastated me, so I got on the road for sixteen hours every three months or so to visit my mother. I loved seeing her face light up as I walked into her room. Prior to losing her ability to speak, I acted silly, making her laugh. She would say, "You crazy Nettie!" She loved for me to massage her hands and feet, and I enjoyed doing it. We would have a dance party. As you know, she loved for me to dance. In the meantime, my other younger sister had been diagnosed with breast cancer, and her prognosis was getting more grim as each day passed, so I would visit with her too.

In February 2009, my sister passed away and left with us her precious and gifted three-year-old son. I say "gifted" because he could read full sentences at the age of two. All kinds of questions were popping up for me then. Who's going to raise him? Will she want me to take him? I was heartbroken that we lost her but even more so that he lost his mother. I found myself eating terribly—things that I hadn't touched in years. And I couldn't seem to stop. That tornado was drawing me near. Each time I tried to pull back and hunt for lower ground, its wind got stronger and eventually whirled me back in.

I made a vow, in spite of my state, to get him as often as I could to spend time with him. Whenever I picked him up, I took him to see momma. She and the other residents loved his visits. You could see her eyes light up, although she couldn't speak. And he loved his grandmother too, often asking me to visit her. For a long time he thought I was his mother because his mother and I looked so much alike. I cried each time it was time for him to go back home to his dad. My sister was gone, but she left us a large presence and present in a little nugget. He brought joy to all of our lives. And he still does.

"It's great that you have him—a part of your sister," my therapist said.

I agree. For years I hosted an annual fundraiser for his college education. My students and I traveled to Louisville to host what we called a FUNky-Fit-a-thon in his honor. But it faded due to lack of support.

"How is the business doing at this time?" she asked.

The crunch of the economic down turn was really squeezing me out. And with it came the new ways of doing business, like, Groupon. I was already losing money with my current business model. Mellenials expected to work out for practically free. But the nail that secured the coffin was the day I walked in, and the water was turned off due to lack of payment (which was not my responsibility). That was my sign to exit stage left. So I said good-bye to that dream, went back to renting a local Park and Rec gym, and moved my equipment to my home where I saw personal training clients. Classes started to build back up.

That is until one day the Park and Rec center manager asked me what kind of history I had with his boss. I replied that I knew her from years back when I rented a facility. But I never had any real "run ins" with her. He said that for some reason she didn't seem to think so because she was trying to cancel my classes.

He was right. It seemed she would do things to actively hurt my business, like take my Thursday classes off the schedule and put them at another facility because, "It's going to be the youth night here, and we need it to be at the time of your class." After transferring my students to another facility and losing half of them in the process, we learned that youth night was never introduced, and on that night the gym would remain empty.

It became the norm for a long time—moving my classes around, canceling classes for no apparent reason, and so on. Finally, after bouncing from center to center (all of which she was in charge) I moved my classes out of Park and Rec for good. No more does someone else have a hold on me and my future. It was truly a blessing in disguise. Praise God for that, in spite of my weight fluctuations!

Death Happens

Dealing with the pain of loss can be debilitating. It's one of the BED risk factors for middle-aged women.

Have you ever lost someone who was close to you?
Who?

How did you deal with the grief?

Have you been able to accept it and move on peacefully?

Resuscitated Memory

It was the year 2010, and I was turning the big fifty. I felt really good at fifty, and folks told me that I looked good too. My new husband took me to Hawaii to celebrate. There we were sitting outside of our beautiful hotel enjoying the wonder of the ocean and the beauty of the mountains. People were walking by, talking and laughing, albeit, life was very serene. The smell of pork was in the air, and his arm was wrapped around my waist.

Out of nowhere, something burst into my mind, and I must've looked as if I'd seen a ghost. I felt like I had confronted a clear and present danger. I broke out in a profuse sweat as if I had encountered a couple of hot flashes all at once. I had an epiphany. I essentially turned into that little eight-year-old girl again. The reencounter of me sitting on the top bunk bed in my room that sat in the long hallway of our ranch home was real. There I was hunkered on the bed with my close family member's finger inside my vagina. I could see his face plain and clear. And there he was, standing in front of me sheepishly looking left and right, making certain that we do not get caught. This I hadn't thought about since it happened. I shared this with my husband, and he just held me tight, which was the only thing he could do for me.

Later in the year I thought about another encounter that I had when I was in middle school. This came out of nowhere as well. I often walked to school by myself because my sister and brother didn't go as much as I did. I loved school and everything about it. I was in the eighth grade. As I walked, a car pulled very close to me. It was a small red car. As I turned to look at what appeared to be close to hitting me, I noticed that there was a white man inside who had his hand wrapped around his penis. It was large and sticking way outside of his pants. As he allowed the car to roll ever so slowly—to the pace of my walk—he continued to stroke it up and down. I was dumbfounded, shocked, and so afraid. It seemed like I watched him entertain me for an hour but in that instant I took off running. From that day forward, I was afraid to walk to school alone although I never told anyone why.

"I'm so sorry these things happened to you. Was this at the time that you were suffering with BED?" my therapist asked.

It baffled me why these two things would hit me at this time in my life. "Wasn't I going through enough?" I thought. My therapist then asked me if I thought it could be a good thing that my past was resurfacing. At the time, I said, "No." But as I write this, I can see that it was because it is helping me to heal—accepting all that has occurred in my life and embracing my whys, whens, whats, wheres, and hows. That embrace has caused me to understand myself better and learn to love myself in spite of the hand that life dealt me, especially the BED.

Resuscitated Memories

According to Wikipedia, repressed memories are memories that have been unconsciously blocked due to the memory being associated with a high level of stress or trauma.

Have you ever had an encounter that was so horrifying that you repressed it from your memory, to have it resurface out of nowhere?

What was it?

Have you ever talked to someone about it or confronted the person or persons for hurting you?

Round In Circles

Momma passed away in November 2012. I listened to "Set Fire to the Rain" by Adele. There were so many songs that reminded me of my momma when I was back in Hopkinsville. When I listened to songs like "My Girl" by the Temptations," "Oh Girl" by The Chi-Lites, "Didn't I (Blow Your Mind This Time)" by The Delfonics, "Stop! In The Name of Love" by The Supremes, and so many more of that era, I was taken back to being that little girl in the living room who showed her and her girlfriends how to dance at the tender age of eight.

It was a sad day, but it was also a relief because it was hard to watch her waste away in that nursing home. And I believe to this day that they were mistreating her but I had no proof. At one point she was admitted to the hospital because her urine was brown. That was enough for me. Based on that fact, there was a meeting called with the nursing home, my sisters, and brothers. I wanted answers, but they seemed to be okay with how momma was being treated. Perhaps they had some relationship with the staff. Our childhood friend worked there for the past twenty years as well. It didn't matter to me. I wanted momma to be cared for properly. So I was glad she wasn't suffering with Alzheimer's and Parkinson's diseases anymore and God was going to be caring for her fully from then on. I was sick of watching her continuously suffer. At first it was her mind to go. Then, of course, the body followed.

"I'm so sorry for your loss." my therapist said.

The time for the funeral preparations came, and my oldest sister, who was power of attorney, talked me into working on the program while she and my other sister did other things. The other things were picking out the clothes that momma would wear, cleaning out her room at the nursing home and tidying up other business. I didn't get to share in those special moments. (The same thing happened with my sister's funeral too.) To make matters worse, after my toiling over the program, just before the funeral began, they gave the funeral director an insert that they had created to place inside the program. I just felt betrayed again. It was disheartening.

I felt like I was in a time warp. They treated me like the bullies in school who threatened to beat me up and the neighbors who cut my arms. For some reason, they just didn't like me. And again, I questioned, why. Could it have something to do with oppression rearing its ugly head? Perhaps it was due to oppression from both our history of being enslaved and our childhood conditions we were raised. My uncle said people felt threatened by my "I'm going to make it" attitude. It always bothered me not to be liked. But it was extra troublesome because they were my sisters.

Around this time my ability to control my weight spun out of control. I've had to move my business two or three more times for various reasons. Although I needed my family more than ever, I pretended not to because I didn't feel as if I could call on them. My aunts were there when I called, but I didn't bother them with too many details. They had enough on their plates. Therefore, I considered my fitness family in Charlotte my family and treated them like that too. I haven't had my sisters to talk to in so long. We didn't know each other. But I longed to be close and I had kept my hopes alive.

For the next two years I would balloon up by twenty pounds and drop down ten of them like a roller coaster—until I hit my wall. Throughout the years I kept telling myself to just do what I did before to lose it. It got to the point where it wasn't even in my head anymore. I couldn't remember what that was. It was too many diets, too many outcomes, and too many times. It was ironic that each time I gained weight, I would look back on when I was ten pounds smaller and think, "And I thought I was big then!"

My therapist said, "You've been through an awful lot in your lifetime. Most people wouldn't have been able to take all that you have and been as successful as you've been. What was your mind supposed to do with all that it's had to endure?"

I appreciated her empathy.

That brick wall that made me call the Renfrew Center was the same wall that saved my life. I called seeking help to get the weight off. But I didn't realize the extent of my problem until I delved into the therapy. I learned that it wasn't about weight at all. It wasn't about what I was eating. It was about what was eating me. But that's the confusion that BED assumes. It's a real battle, and it tricks you into thinking it's about the bulge. As well, life is a battle—one that we cannot stop fighting for.

Round In Circles

There are several reasons why a growing number of African American women (and men) feel their body isn't ideal, although only 5 percent of the American population naturally possess the body types often portrayed. Why then is 95 percent of the population killing themselves to look like 5 percent?

Do you often compare yourself to the women (or men) you see in the media, or others with whom you come in contact?

If you think you may have an eating disorder, what professional help are you seeking and from whom?

What things do you do on a regular basis to make you feel good about yourself? List them.

Recovery

I spent the next couple of months in one-on-one and group therapy, growing and learning to understand my binge-eating disorder and eating disorders in general. It was a struggle to get me out of my own head. But I wanted to get better. Eventually I learned to accept the fact that a clothing size doesn't define my character or my knowledge of fitness and health, although many people feel that it should. I decided to love myself regardless of my scale number, and I believed that tomorrow would bring a new day with new hope and new light.

I learned that television ads and magazines had a defining effect on me and that I allowed them to determine the standard of beauty for all women (and men). I came to know that that had to stop!

I learned to pamper myself and love every inch of me—bulges, cellulite, stretch marks, scars, and all. Have I lost the weight that I had gained? No. But although my body is the same, it's my mind that's different.

Recovery is something I will be in for the rest of my life. I would rather be in recovery than in that dark, scary, unknown dungeon from which I came. For me It is the fight of all fights and the battle of all battles.

But first I had to get to the bottom of what was causing the behavior. I knew it wasn't the good things in my life. It was the hard times that I tried to forget about, the stuff in the back of my mind that I had suppressed for decades. Those were the things that needed to be recovered, resurfaced, and dealt with.

There are times that I get the urge to binge again, and at times I look up, and I've already done it. The difference is that I can recognize it and control it, and I don't feel defeated because I did it. I also know what my triggers (things that initiate the action of binging) are, like stress and anxiety.

Now, instead of helplessly running toward the tornado, knowing that I will be swooped up and spin out of control, I can resist it. Being addicted to food is likened to being addicted to drugs, alcohol, or shopping. It's the same concept of addiction, except you don't have to consume drugs or alcohol to live. You do, however, have to eat.

I still have to work out twice as hard as others to just maintain my weight due to my thyroid issue and the years of yo-yo dieting. I don't, however, feel like I have to be on "one hundred" all the time. Sure, I get anxiety about my weight gain, but it doesn't become all consuming, and I don't allow it to define me. I no longer wonder why I wasn't born with a silver spoon in my mouth or wish that I looked like someone else.

My husband once said, "You never want to be like someone else, because you get all of them: Their issues, their pain and sorrows. And you never know what their struggles might be. Oftentimes it's worse than yours." He didn't know, but the first time he said it, I was wishing I looked like someone else. It helped me in my recovery.

Sometimes it's hard to accept the cards you've been dealt. I often wonder if I would have an eating disorder if my childhood, adolescence, and adulthood had not been the way they were. Maybe or maybe not. I will never know the answer to that question. But with self-discovery, self-awareness, self-care and self-love, we can make it through the storms and better understand them too. Together, this awareness provides self-acceptance, and that's the greatest tool in the shed. It liberates you and leads to forgiveness for yourself and for those who may have contributed to your pain. In my eyes, forgiveness is the reliever of deep emotional pain.

I have been fortunate to help thousands of African American women realize their full potential through fitness. It saved my life too. Recently, in a movie that I was watching, the actress said something that was profound to me: "Those who have been hurt the worst have the ability to heal the most." Perhaps my rise and fall from the weight-loss grace was so I could help those struggling with BED as well. After all, that's why I've shared my story.

Hopefully you can see that through therapy, I learned how I got there—to BED. Your battle may be totally different from mine. I encourage you, however, to search your heart and soul, seek therapy, and find your way to take cover from the whirling tornado that exists within.

If you are someone who suffers in silence from this disease, my heart reaches out to you. The guilt and shame that comes alongside it can be debilitating in and of itself. Through all that I've been through (good and bad), I can see light at the end of the tunnel. I'm not out of the tunnel; it's not going anywhere. But I'm continuing to fight to get through it not only for myself but for the many African American women (and men) who suffer in silence like I did.

My goals are short and sweet. They are to continue with therapy, to take the time out to love all of me while keeping in mind that it is my mind and not my mirror that defines me. In other words, I am my own sexy. I choose to rely on God above and my solid circle of family and friends below. I am reconstructing my life on my own terms, from the inside out.

Thank you for reading my story.

Please review your answers throughout the book to determine if you should seek help for Binge Eating Disorder. There is help available, but you must take the first step to get it. If you would like to explore the help of the Renfrew Center, please call 1-800-RENFREW or log on to www.renfrewcenter.com.

Nettie Reeves is a fitness, life, and health coach who advises around the world. What began as a desire to help an individual's health grew into a lifelong passion to improve the quality of others' lives by leading, motivating, teaching, and sharing her story. She is the creator of Nettie Reeves's FUNky Fit, which has been a fitness force in communities across the country over the past twenty years. Her mantra is "The mind, not the mirror, is the judge." Nettie holds a BA in communications and many certifications in the health and fitness arena. She has won numerous awards for her work, including the Steve Harvey Hoodie (Neighborhood) Award and the President Obama's Council on Fitness and Nutrition Award. She is the proud wife of Eric Lewis and mother to Daniel Guess Jr. Contact her at nettie@nshapewithn.com